Presented to:

....

*Teaching is the profession that teaches
all the other professions.*

UNKNOWN

Presented by:

....

Date:

....

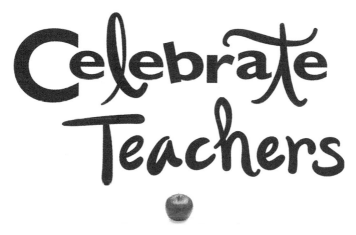

Celebrate Teachers

*Heartwarming Stories, Inspirational Sayings, and
Meaningful Expressions for Teachers*

WHITE STONE BOOKS
LAKELAND, FLORIDA

Celebrate Teachers:
Heartwarming Stories, Inspirational Sayings,
and Meaningful Expressions for Teachers

ISBN 1-59379-092-9

Copyright © 2006 Bordon Books, Tulsa, OK
Product developed by Bordon Books
Published by White Stone Books
P.O. Box 2835
Lakeland, Florida 33806

Manuscript written and compiled by SnapdragonGroup℠ Editorial Services.

Contents

The dream begins with

a teacher who believes

in you....

DAN RATHER

Former CBS Evening News Anchor from 1981-2005

Introduction

Teaching is more than a skill. It is a God-given gift. You either have it or you don't.

Teaching is a life—a profession like no other. The investment a teacher makes is far-reaching and requires stellar dedication. Any teacher will tell you there are days when he or she has been tempted to cut and run, never to return. But that feeling passes the instant a long-awaited understanding appears on the face of a student, or when a former student drops by to say, "Thank you for opening my mind to new ideas." The life of a teacher is all that and more.

Celebrate Teachers was inspired by the gifted teachers who have touched each of our lives. It could have been a high school teacher, a mentor, a coach, or even a Sunday school leader, but each sparked a special flame in the heart and mind that changed our life course for the better.

For these life-changers, we applaud you. No matter where you serve, you are remembered and celebrated.

As you read the pages of this book, we hope you will celebrate with us!

The art of teaching is the art of assisting discovery.

MARK VAN DOREN

American Poet, Critic, and Educator

1894–1972

Exceptional Teachers Are ... Creative and Resourceful.

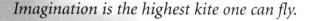

Imagination is the highest kite one can fly.

LAUREN BACALL

American Film and Stage Actress

Better than a thousand days
of diligent study
is one day with a great teacher.

JAPANESE PROVERB

I love to teach.

I love to teach as a painter loves to paint,

as a musician loves to play,

as a singer loves to sing,

as a strong man rejoices to run a race.

Teaching is an art.

WILLIAM PHELPS

American Educator and Literary Critic

1865–1943

11

Keeping the creative spark in your teaching
takes effort. The exciting thing is, though, that God
is the Master Creator; and He never runs out
of ideas. Look to Him to inspire you and help you
make the most of the resources He's provided.

🌴

Mountain-Shaper! Wind-Maker!
. . . [God] brings everything out of nothing,
like dawn out of darkness.

AMOS 4:13 MSG

Effective Bulletin Boards

Don't be afraid to express yourself when it comes to your bulletin boards. Spice up your room by trying a different approach or look.

- Take pictures of the students and school activities and post them.

- Use wrapping paper, cloth, or lace for the background.

- Use it as a "message center" for your students.

- Post assignments.

- Use 3-D items such as cornstalks or toy spaceships to accent a theme.

- Color, color, color.

- Make your own cutouts using copies from a book or the computer. You can trace them onto the bulletin board with the help of an overhead projector.

- Use twisted brown butcher paper to make a vine-like border.

- Be creative and have fun![1]

Heavenly Father,

Thank You for the gift of creativity. I know that Your desire is that the whole of creation would reflect Your glory.

So as I stretch my creative wings and try new things, let the work of my hands honor You.

Help me to inspire my students with the courage to try new things, as well. Help me lead them beyond the fears that might hold them back and toward the individual gifts You have placed inside each and every one of them.

Amen.

A+

Hidden Talents

Alison was tiny, quiet, and as close to invisible as a child could be. She had moved eleven times before the fourth grade, and her actions toward the other children let me know she had little or no hope of forming any long-lasting friendships here either. Alison did poor work, but she did not qualify for any of the myriad of special programs in our district.

Two-thirds of my class that year was composed of wild, boisterous boys. I was afraid Alison would disappear altogether in that group, so I asked God for wisdom. I felt impressed to put Alison with a group of my most outspoken boys. I made her the "captain" of the group and told her and all the other captains what I wanted them to accomplish.

Alison took her role very seriously and began to organize the boys to complete the job at hand. They laughed and joked at first, but Alison dropped her arms and stared silently at them until they complied. She never said a word; she just waited. I would not have taken her for a leader by any means, but there she was—organized, working ahead of schedule—and the boys had never been better behaved or more on task.

Alison's group presentation was far superior to that of any other group in the room. It was uncharacteristically neat, detailed, and imaginative. When commenting on this in class, I asked to what she attributed her great success. She said, "You made me the captain. That means you think I am smart. No one has ever thought I was smart before, so I prayed for Jesus to make me smart."[2]

Do you have an Alison in your class? If so, ask God to give you creative ways to draw out that student's God-given gifts and talents. Assign a special task today, and voice your confidence to that student, encouraging him or her every step of the way.

I Am Creative and Resourceful...

Because of the gifts God has placed in me, I'm eager to use them in creative ways to help my students. I'm confident that if I need fresh ideas, I can turn to God for a never-ending supply. I thank Him that as I present my lessons in bold, new ways, my students will become excited about learning and ready to stretch their own creative wings.

A+

Ways to Renew Your Spirit

All creativity comes directly or indirectly from the great Creator—God. Keep the embers of creativity hot by making these simple spiritual practices part of your day.

❋ *Start the day with prayer.*

Spending your first few waking minutes with God—asking for guidance, wisdom, and patience—is the best way to start your day off right. But don't stop there. Throughout the day, continue asking God for what you need, and remember to thank Him for refreshing you with His presence.

❋ *On breaks, read your Bible.*

Keep a Bible on a classroom shelf so you can turn to it for inspiration to help revitalize your spirit for the remainder of the day.

❋ *Just for today, give your cares to God.*

It can be difficult to let go of everything and trust in God. Decide to step away from the concern for just one day. It will give you a break and recharge your batteries for the days ahead.

Inspiration and creativity are fragile commodities, especially for teachers, among whom burnout rates are high. Use these practical activities to let your mind "breathe" and to rejuvenate your creative instincts.

❦ *Find some quiet time.*

Sometimes it helps to have some silent time alone—away from shuffling papers and grinding pencil sharpeners. Your car may be the perfect place.

❦ *Eat lunch outside.*

Of course you can't do this on days when the weather is inclement, but nothing lifts the spirits like enjoying the beauty of nature with its many sights and sounds.

❦ *Get away for a retreat or other function.*

Break the routine of your life. Introduce some adventure into your world, as well as a change of scenery. It can be very energizing to meet new people who share common interests. You may even make a new friend or two!

❦ *Do an anonymous kind deed for someone.*

It is indeed more blessed to give than to receive. It fills your heart with joy.[3]

When I am ...

completely myself ...

it is on such occasions that

my ideas flow best and

most abundantly.

WOLFGANG AMADEUS MOZART

European Composer

1756–1791

Creativity is so delicate a flower
that praise tends to make it bloom,
while discouragement often nips it in the bud.
Any of us will put out more and
better ideas if our efforts are appreciated.

ALEX F. OSBORN

Advertising Executive—

Helped Coin the Term "Brainstorming"

1888–1966

Teaching is a partnership with God.
You are not molding iron nor
chiseling marble; you are working with the
Creator of the universe in shaping human
character and determining destiny.

RUTH VAUGHN

Author and Playwright

The secret of education is respecting the pupil.

RALPH WALDO EMERSON

American Writer, Speaker, and Poet

1803–1882

Exceptional Teachers Are ...
Fair and Wise.

I long to put the experience of fifty years
at once into your young lives, to give you at
once the key to that treasure chamber
every gem of which has cost me tears and
struggles and prayers, but you must work
for these inward treasures yourselves.

HARRIET BEECHER STOWE

Abolitionist Author of *Uncle Tom's Cabin*

1811–1896

23

It takes wisdom to know how to be fair to your students.
But a feeling of equality is a wonderful gift
you can give them. It allows them the freedom to relax
and do their best, without fear
of being misjudged or misunderstood.

🌴

Incline your ear to wisdom,
And apply your heart to understanding.

PROVERBS 2:2 NKJV

Engaging Students in Classroom Participation

The more participation you can have out of a class, the more your students will remember about the discussion. Involving students in the learning process is a great way to guarantee the retention of the lesson.

♣ *Form "tribes."*

Establish tribes by setting desks into groups. Each tribe creates its own name and team flag. Allow the tribes to work on specific assignments, and make each group responsible for the behavior of its members. Tally points on a bulletin board for each tribe, and reward the winning group. The positive peer pressure can serve as a great incentive for improving grades and class behavior.

♣ *Allow students to participate in decision-making.*

Students don't mind following the rules if they feel they have had a hand in establishing them.

♣ *Vary the media in your classroom.*

Students learn in a variety of ways and respond to diversity. Use that to your advantage. Different forms of media can produce better retention of the subject matter. Examples include newspapers, videos, the Internet, magazines, and special guest speakers.[4]

Heavenly Father,

It's tough sometimes knowing how to handle situations fairly. All of my students are valuable and deserve my best. Help me avoid the temptation to favor certain students over others—help me deal with all of my students equally.

Give me Your wisdom and help me to respond to challenges carefully and prayerfully, without drawing conclusions. As I turn to You for wisdom, I know You will be there to guide me in every situation.

Amen.

A+

A Tough Little Philly in Texas

The first time I saw Terrie's mother, she came out literally kicking and screaming, as a couple of policemen escorted her out of the elementary school. She was a fireball from "Philly," and our little Texas town had never seen the likes of her.

Parent/teacher conference night soon followed, and I dreaded the encounter. I earnestly sought the Lord about it because I was genuinely concerned about Terrie, yet I didn't want a repeat performance from her mother. The following day I sensed God leading me to handle the conference assertively.

"Hi! I'm Mrs. Davis. I've been so anxious to meet you," I said cheerfully as I came from behind my desk to greet her. "Let me close this door, so we can really talk." Before she could start in with her usual discourse, I said, "It is so encouraging when parents care about their kids and keep tabs on them like you do. Now," I continued, hardly drawing a breath, "I need your advice. After all, no one knows Terrie better than you, right?"

She nodded and sat staring at me.

"I need your input on the best way to handle her when she disrupts class or doesn't complete her assignments." I sat ready to take notes.

Taken aback, she stammered a bit before she began listing consequences she felt I could use. She ended by patting me on the knee and assuring me that if Terrie didn't do exactly as I told her, I was to let her know and she would take care of it.

Things began to turn around for Terrie, and from that day until this, whenever I see her mother, she greets me and begins talking like we are old friends. The wisdom of God works wonders.[5]

Think of some ways to improve your parent/teacher conferences and jot them down for later reference. Ask God to give you wisdom in your dealings with difficult people including your students, their parents, and members of the faculty.

I Am Fair and Wise...

I look to God for help as I make wise decisions in my classroom. When I need more wisdom, I know God will be there to guide the way. Because of this, I know my students will be able to trust in the fact that I'm a fair teacher. If conflicts arise, I will believe the best about my students. In every situation, I will reassure them that their personal growth and happiness are my highest concerns.

A+

TIPS FOR SUCCESSFUL PARENT/TEACHER CONFERENCES

There is no need to fear a parent/teacher conference. Use this time to get the parents on the same page with you. Making allies out of the parents can improve life in the classroom.

🌴 *Exhibit a positive and upbeat disposition.*

This will go a long way in disarming angry parents. Often loud and aggressive people just need to feel they are being heard. Make it clear that you are on the same team working with them for the benefit of their child.

🌴 *Begin with something positive.*

Conferences are difficult for parents as well. Begin by acknowledging the strengths of their child, and then slowly move into areas that need improvement.

🌴 *Stick to the facts.*

Tell the parents about the situation concerning their child, and allow them to make the obvious conclusions.

🌴 *Have all documentation and paperwork available.*

Always bring your grade book, samples of the child's work, and any significant paperwork to the meeting with you. Write down items that require follow-up.

🌴 *Don't surprise parents with grades.*

Parents should be aware of their child's progress long before the end of the term. Contact parents when grades first begin to slip. If a parent doesn't know there is a problem, he or she can't help solve it.

🌳 *Stay on the subject.*

Although it is important to establish a rapport with parents, stay in control of the discussion.

🌳 *Offer potential solutions.*

By presenting ideas that could benefit their child, you increase the chances of having parental support at home. Have available a list of tutors, or offer to send home extra study sheets and/or projects for grade recovery or improvement.

🌳 *Don't overwhelm parents with information.*

Parents often come straight from work to a conference and are frequently exhausted from the day. Simplify as much as possible. Written examples are tremendously effective and are great to send home after the discussion.

🌳 *Stick to time schedules.*

Begin on time, be prepared, and finish on time. If information has not been covered due to time restraints, then schedule a second appointment with the intent to "follow up on progress." Not only will parents appreciate your respect for their time, but you will more likely secure follow-through on future scheduled meetings if it is perceived that you anticipate positive resolve.

🌳 *Create a nonthreatening environment.*

Instead of sitting behind your desk, sit next to the parents at a table. This will foster a sense of camaraderie and help put the parents at ease.[6]

WISE WAYS TO SIMPLIFY YOUR LIFE

Sometimes the simplest things can make life and your classroom run more smoothly.

- ### *Clean out and organize your desk.*

  Clutter triggers stress, so don't just stack those papers on the corner of your desk. Sift through them and throw away or file what you won't need immediately.

- ### *Make all of your copies one day ahead of time.*

  One trip to the copier is better than fifty. Tab all your books with the necessary pages and make the copies all at once. You can even plan ahead and make your copies for other lessons, keeping any leftovers in the book for later use.

- ### *Stick to one day-planner.*

  You need not keep a separate day-planner for every class, car, or desk. One should be sufficient to handle your personal responsibilities, as well as those for the school. The key is to get one large enough and flexible enough to adapt to various aspects of your life's routines. Keep it simple.

- ### *Don't sweat the small stuff.*

  Don't worry about becoming "Super Teacher." With experience you will discover the things that work best for you.

🌿 *Schedule a day to leave on time and stick to it.*

Though the bell may ring at 3:00 P.M., we all know that teachers do not get off work then. Select a day that you would like to leave earlier than usual and then stick to it. Not everything has to be done in the classroom, and a change of scenery might be just what you need.

🌿 *Open mail close to a wastebasket.*

Toss junk mail into file thirteen the minute you open it. For bills, discard the outer envelopes along with any unwanted inserts. Establish a designated place for coupons and special offers.

🌿 *Avoid subscribing to things you don't have time to read.*

Mailboxes fill up with a vast variety of catalogs and magazines, leading to a cluttered desk and guilt over good intentions. Only subscribe to what you know you can read, and free your mind for more productive and rewarding matters!

🌿 *Avoid getting involved in unnecessary school politics.*

Politics are everywhere; when feasible, steer clear of getting involved. You will save yourself stress and pointless worry.[7]

What nobler employment, or more
valuable to the state, than that of the man
who instructs the rising generation.

MARCUS TULLIUS CICERO

Roman Statesman, Orator, and Author

106–43 B.C.

Wisdom is the right use of knowledge.
To know is not to be wise.
Many men know a great deal and are all
the greater fools for it. To know how
to use knowledge is to have wisdom.

CHARLES SPURGEON
Preacher, Theologian, and Author
1834-1892

🌴

There's nothing better than being wise,
Knowing how to interpret the meaning of life.
Wisdom puts light in the eyes,
And gives gentleness to words and manners.

ECCLESIASTES 8:1 MSG

🌴

The art of being wise is the art of knowing
what to overlook.

WILLIAM JAMES
American Philosopher
1842-1910

Man is never nearer the Divine than in his compassionate moments.

JOSEPH H. HERTZ

Chief Rabbi of the British Empire

1872–1946

Exceptional Teachers Are ... Tenderhearted and Compassionate.

🌴

There never was any heart truly
great and generous, that was not also
tender and compassionate.

ROBERT FROST

American Poet

1874–1963

If I can stop one Heart from breaking

I shall not live in vain.

If I can ease one Life the Aching

Or cool one Pain

Or help one fainting Robin

Upon his Nest again

I shall not live in Vain.

EMILY DICKINSON

American Poet

1830–1886

I expect to pass through life but once.

If, therefore, there be any kindness

I can show, or any good thing I can do

to any fellow being,

let me do it now, and not defer or neglect it,

as I shall not pass this way again.

WILLIAM PENN

Quaker and Founder of Pennsylvania

1644–1718

39

Perhaps being tenderhearted is second nature to you.

Or maybe you have to work at it a bit.

Either way, as you operate in kindness and compassion

toward your students, you'll reap the rewards of closer,

more trusting relationships.

The LORD is like a father to his children,
tender and compassionate to those who fear him.

PSALM 103:13 NLT

Classroom Management

If you manage your classroom well, you'll spend much less time investing in damage control and navigating through challenging situations. You'll have more time to be sensitive to your students' emotional needs. Consider instituting these steps.

❧ *Assign jobs to students.*

Tasks may not get completed as well as if you did them yourself, but you will have less to think about. Giving students responsibility can be incredibly valuable as it strengthens self-esteem. Your students will also begin to take pride in their classroom and feel as though they have become an integral part of the system.

❧ *Create a platform to air out problems privately.*

Challenges will arise between students. Having a known and prearranged platform for students to air out their concerns will eliminate unnecessary discord in the classroom. Try having students inform you when a problem is perceived and set up a meeting time in a neutral environment where you can act as a mediator.

❧ *Make available a suggestion/problem box.*

Some students may feel intimidated about offering creative ideas or informing you about a dilemma. Having the opportunity to share these things anonymously is less threatening and will help them feel more comfortable to share honestly.[8]

Heavenly Father,

Help me to keep a heart of compassion. Even on the days when I feel worn and impatient with my students, help me keep sight of why I wanted to teach in the first place.

Father, keep me aware of the needs of these children who depend on me. I want to be a safe harbor my students can turn to. As I reach out to them with tenderness, I pray that they'll be drawn to Your love. Help me to always look at my students through Your eyes of compassion.

Amen.

Learning to Trust Again

A fter school one day, I found Amy crying uncontrollably in the bathroom. When I asked her what was wrong, she blurted out the story of how her older sister, Beth, had been killed in a car accident the year before. She said she had been angry at God for a long time, and that because of it, she was no longer participating in her Bible study or going to church. She wanted to know why God had let her sister die.

I pulled Amy close and, looking deep into her eyes, explained that God loved her and Beth very much and that He was also heartbroken over the loss.

"It's not that Beth sinned, but there is sin in this world and bad things happen to good people, Amy. But know that one day we will be reunited with our loved ones in heaven. There will be no more death or tears," I soothed.

Drying her tears, Amy began to tell me about Beth and what a wonderful person she was and how active she had been in church and youth activities.

I said, "It sounds like Beth loved Jesus very much and that she lived her life for Him. What do you think she would say to you if she knew you had given up on God?"

"She would be disappointed. She'd probably tell me that I should trust God, that someday I would understand."

Eventually Amy did regain her love and trust in the Lord, and today she is very involved in her church and several outreach programs. She has even begun an outreach for young people who have lost loved ones, using her experience to console others and inspire renewed hope.

Establish a relationship of trust with your students by assuring them that they can come and speak to you privately and confidentially about the things that are troubling them. Tell them today.[9]

I Am Tenderhearted and Compassionate...

Because of God's great compassion toward me, I can extend that same compassion toward my students. I am becoming all that God created me to be, every day, with every student. I am thankful to God for the tender heart He has given me toward the students He has placed in my care.

A+

SETTING THE STANDARD

Raise the bar at your school and in your classroom. Teaching is a profession that deserves respect and trust. When your students respect you, they will be more inclined to open up to you, making you more aware of their needs and better able to reach out to them.

❦ *Dress professionally.*

Students and others will relate to you according to how you carry yourself and the manner in which you dress.

❦ *Make eye contact and really listen.*

Just as you expect to have the full attention of your class, be sure to set the example and give them that same respect in your dealings with them.

❦ *Exercise good manners.*

Using phrases such as "Thank you," "You're welcome," and "Please" establishes a courteous atmosphere and sets the example for your students to follow. Proper etiquette reflects a respect for others, and it is a life skill that will benefit your students long after they leave the walls of your classroom.

❦ *Be an encourager.*

Listening to and encouraging your students will go a long way in building self-esteem and a sense of personal worth. You may be the only person to give your students positive feedback on a given day.

🌴 *Praise publicly; reprimand privately.*

Praising your students publicly will instill a positive self-image; and by reprimanding in private, you preserve the students' dignity and prevent the damaging effects of humiliation.

🌴 *Don't engage in teachers' lounge gossip.*

Although the lounge can be a source of creative ideas and inspiration, it can also be a breeding ground for negativity. Gossip serves only to hurt and offend others. If gossip is plaguing your lounge, save yourself the mental energy and walk away.

🌴 *Refrain from interrupting students.*

By doing this, you show your students the same respect you expect them to exhibit toward you. Wait until they are finished speaking before interjecting any comments or questions.

🌴 *Never leave the classroom unsupervised.*

Too many accidents can happen when a teacher leaves the room. Send a reliable student to find an adult to watch your class while you step out for a few minutes.

🌴 *Have business cards available.*

Not only will this reflect professionalism on your part, it will enable parents to get in touch with you quickly and as needed. Include the contact information of your choice, such as your home telephone number, cell phone number, and e-mail address. With a computer, you can even create your own business cards, using precut card stock made for that purpose.[10]

Self-sacrifice is never entirely unselfish,

for the giver never fails to receive.

DOLORES E. MCGUIRE

Author

Exceptional Teachers Are ... Selfless and Sacrificial.

A good teacher is like a candle—
it consumes itself
to light the way for others.

ANONYMOUS

God make my life a little light,
Within the world to glow;
A tiny flame that burneth bright
Wherever I may go.

God make my life a little flower,
That giveth joy to all,
Content to bloom in native bower,
Although its place be small.

God make my life a little staff,
Whereon the weak may rest,
That so what health and strength I have
May serve my neighbors best.

MATILDA BETHAM-EDWARDS

Real fulfillment in your life
will come from striving
with all of your physical and spiritual
might for a worthwhile objective
that helps others and is
larger than your self-interest.

GEORGE J. MITCHELL

Maine Senator

It goes against society's norms to be sacrificial and selfless.
Yet, out of our love for God, we're compelled to do so.
If you struggle with this area, look to Him for help, for
He truly understands the importance of putting others first.

🌴

Each of you should look not only to your own interests,
but also to the interests of others.
Your attitude should be the same as that of Christ Jesus:
Who, …
made himself nothing,
taking the very nature of a servant.

PHILIPPIANS 2:4–7

Recharging Your Batteries

Teaching is not for wimps. It means giving and giving and giving some more. Try one of these strategies for a quick fix to get you through the rest of the day:

- Have a cup of specialty coffee or your favorite soft drink.

- Play some fun music and sing along.

- Read something motivational by one of your favorite authors.

- Step outside and get a quick breath of fresh air. Breathe deeply and take in the beauty of God's creation.

- If it's not your day for lunch duty, find a quiet place and take a quick power nap.[11]

Heavenly Father,

Teaching can be overwhelming some days. The demands seem endless, and I often find my strength waning. It is easy to become more focused on myself rather than the needs of my students.

I want to have a servant's heart like Jesus—to put my students first and let go of the daily cares that would distract me. Help me to do that, Father. Infuse me with Your grace and strength so that I can invest my best, always.

Thank You for Your guidance each day as I invest my heart into my students and use the gifts You have placed in me for their benefit.

Amen.

A Day to Treasure

Sometimes the truly sacrificial nature of someone's actions can be seen only in hindsight.

When my oldest daughter, Katie, was in the fifth grade, her teacher, Jim Craig, pulled her and another student, Jenny, out into the hallway one day. He asked them if they'd like to go horseback riding at his daughter's ranch that weekend. From the way their faces lit up, it was evident what their answers would be. When asked for permission, both sets of parents agreed to the outing.

Mr. Craig knew that both girls loved horses. Katie had been bitten by the riding bug that previous year and had taken lessons at a nearby stable, helping to pay for her lessons by cleaning the stables and grooming the horses. She'd even ridden in several horse shows. But to have the luxury of riding a horse all day—without having to muck out a stall, no less!—was a real treat.

That weekend, Mr. Craig and some other teachers picked

up the girls and drove them to his daughter's ranch. The girls spent a memorable day riding the horses, eating fried chicken, and swinging on the tire swing in the barn. When Katie came home at the end of the day, she was tired but happy. What a marvelous gift her teacher had given her!

It was only a year later that Mr. Craig died of cancer.

I've thought of his gift to Katie often over the years since then. Was he aware of his condition as he sacrificed a full day of the last year of his life? Was he in pain, even as he smiled at the girls on the horses and posed for pictures with them? The photos we have of that day reveal nothing but the pure joy of a teacher standing proudly with his students. Perhaps he understood, better than most of us, that to fully live involves putting others first—that to die to ourselves really is, in the end, what it means to live.[12]

In everything I did, I showed you
that by this kind of hard work
we must help the weak,
remembering the words the Lord Jesus
himself said: "It is more blessed
to give than to receive."

ACTS 20:35

Survival Kits

The Teacher's Survival Kit

Keep this kit close at hand. Some items to put in it might include: aspirin, antacids, cough drops, breath mints, wet wipes, bandages, antibacterial lotion, a needle and thread, safety pins, nail file, nail clippers, a tube of Super Glue, a small toothbrush and toothpaste, a comb and mirror, feminine products, deodorant, clear nail polish for runs in pantyhose, an extra pair of pantyhose, correct change for vending machines, an extra car door key, and even a small tool set.

Survival Kit for Substitute Teachers

Always have this kit pinned on the wall by your desk, flagged in big bold letters. In the event that you must be absent unexpectedly, it should contain all the vital information any sub would need:

* a personal note welcoming the substitute, along with an inspirational bookmark as a token gift

* a list of class helpers

* any health issues of students

* seating charts

* emergency information sheet: fire drill routes, nurse contact information, location of first-aid kit

* list of class rules

* master copies of various assignments and review pages

* incentives for good behavior, such as special books or videos, to be used at the end of the day

ORGANIZATIONAL AIDS

♣ *Avoid possible accusations by picking up all the papers and stapling them together.*

At some point, every teacher has heard, "You lost my paper!" To avoid this, grade and record the papers while they are still stapled, and do not pull apart until you are ready to return them. In addition, if you assign a number to each of your students, you will know immediately if a page is missing.

♣ *Keep a schedule notebook.*

If you find yourself in a situation where you teach many different classes on differing days, it might be wise to keep a schedule notebook. Take a three-ring binder and use dividers to separate into different days. In plastic sheet protectors, put a schedule of your classes under each section. Also include a list of class rules, fire drill information, and intercom numbers. Include a diagram of your room with a seating chart for each class.

♣ *Keep your students organized.*

Start by making each student a colored folder for each of the classes you teach. In each folder, they can keep blank paper and returned work. When it is time to study for a test, all of their work is already in the folder for them to review. After each chapter, clean out the folders and start over again.[13]

Whenever we do what we can,
we immediately can do more.

JAMES FREEMAN CLARKE
American Clergyman, Author, Editor
1810–1888

Bringing the Classroom to Life

Freshen up your classroom and bring new life indoors by utilizing some of these simple ideas:

- Open the window.

- Place live plants in various spots around the room.

- Adopt a classroom pet.

- Light a scented candle, or put out fresh potpourri.

- Play soft classical music in the background.

- Hang posters, piñatas, mobiles, planets, airplane models, or any other fun objects from the ceiling.[14]

We blossom under praise like flowers in sun and dew;

we open, we reach, we grow.

GERHARD E. FROST
Christian Author

Exceptional Teachers Are ... Encouraging and Supportive.

Children require guidance and sympathy
far more than instruction.

ANNIE SULLIVAN

Teacher of Helen Keller

1866–1936

It feels good to be a cheerleader for a student, doesn't it?
To see the smiles that come to their faces when you encourage
and support them. Perhaps, even more than imparting
knowledge, your most important task as a teacher is to show
that you believe in them and to let them know that someone's
watching—and clapping wildly—as they cross that finish line.

Be devoted to one another in brotherly love.
Honor one another above yourselves.

ROMANS 12:10

Celebrating the Gifts and Strengths of Your Students

Encourage your students to share their gifts and talents to enhance the classroom environment and to help them develop their strong points.

🌸 *Openly praise.*

People who are praised openly tend to work harder and are more devoted to those who compliment them. This can build self-confidence and help minimize undesirable behavior.

🌸 *Create a personal notebook.*

Have your students decorate the outside of a paper report folder, the type with three clasps and a pocket inside each cover. Then, have each student write three to five positive comments about each person in the class. Encourage them to avoid such clichés as "You are nice" and "You are sweet." The students then insert all of the comments written about them into their individual books. It is a great way for class members to bond, as well as reduce challenges with peer pressure and minimize conflict. It is sure to become a lifelong, treasured item.

🌸 *Have a "Star Student" of the week.*

Choose one or two students every week to be "Star Students." Hang their pictures on a bulletin board with lists of things such as their favorite activities, foods, colors, and songs. They can also be the "special helpers" during this period of time.[15]

Heavenly Father,

I want to have a lasting influence on my students. I want the words I speak to have an impact.

Father, I want to be known as a supporter and an encourager. Show me ways that I can support the dreams of my students. Let the words I speak impart life and empower them to become all that You've planned for them to be. Let every word I speak to them be a word worth remembering—a word that will influence them for good, long after they leave my classroom.

Amen.

A+

Zola Helen Ross: An Expert and an Encourager

Z ola Helen Ross taught Advanced Fiction Writing at an adult trade school in the Seattle area. Gruff, sturdy, and plain-spoken, she seemed a perfect fit for a trade school, even though a fiction writing course seemed misplaced there.

Students in her class were required to have at least one novel published by a reputable publisher. A writer friend suggested, "Maybe you can get in on the strength of your creative writing degree."

I tried and, to my surprise, was accepted for the Wednesday evening class.

On the first night, Mrs. Ross introduced my friend and told about her book in print. Next, she introduced me and mentioned my degree in creative writing. Most of the students had five or six novels published, and one had seventeen novels to her credit. Several eyed me dubiously, as if to say, "What are you doing here? It took us years of struggle to be admitted into this class."

I tried to look confident.

When asked what I was writing, I said, "I'm not sure."

It was a Wednesday night class of fifteen or so students, both men and women. Mrs. Ross would read a student's chapter or short story aloud, then the students critiqued, one by one, around the long table.

Some comments were harsh such as, "Your characters aren't worth caring about," or "You've ruined your suspense," or "The story is too long-winded." Nevertheless, all advice from this group was worth considering.

After attending several classes, I wrung a story out of my heart. The next Wednesday night, I gathered my courage and the latest draft of "A Time to Decide," and submitted it to the class. My classmates ripped into it—and my shaky confidence. I took notes, a good excuse to keep my head down and not meet their eyes. Criticism of my work hurt then.

The next week, Mrs. Ross returned my story with her notes. Her words were the driving force of my career. "You have the talent. Let's see if you can take constructive criticism."

At home, I rewrote the story as she suggested, then returned it to her.

This time, after reading it, she said, "Send it to the fiction editor at *Good Housekeeping* and tell them I told you to send it."

I did.

The editor wrote, "We like the story, but can you cut it to 1,400 words?"

Lop off more than half? It was 3,600 words.

Impossible!

In class, Mrs. Ross said, "It's a worthwhile learning experience for you."

A worthwhile learning experience?

Finally, determination to publish won out. I cut it to 1,400 words.

She reread it and wrote, "You've done it!"

It sold to *Good Housekeeping* and then to magazines in forty other countries. It was the first of my short stories published by them, and I clearly owed that success to Mrs. Ross.

Eventually, she taught a fiction writing course at the University of Washington. It was quite a leap, from trade school to a university.

For her, an advanced degree was unnecessary. She had written fifty-five novels, all published, some under male pseudonyms in the days when women didn't write westerns or historicals. Indeed, when women wrote very little.

Mrs. Ross knew the New York publishing scene and was determined that her students would get their writing published. Many of us did, thanks to her advice and encouragement.

Unfortunately, we moved away, and I no longer had her guidance. I struggled on by myself, missing her and trying to remember what she'd taught us. "Cut this paragraph ... flesh out this character ... what's the real theme? ... you've begun the story too soon."

Over the years, she was eager to hear about my thirty-six novels being published—and she promoted them, as well. I missed her. No one, including my university professors, had ever helped and encouraged me so much.

When I became a Christian, she continued to read my novels, and I pray that they touched her heart.

Twenty years later, I returned to the Seattle area and took her out for lunch. She was frail and used a walker, but her knack for encouraging remained. "Keep on writing," she told me in her dear gruff voice. "You're going to make it big."

"If it weren't for you," I answered with tears in my eyes, "I'd never have become a writer at all."

She frowned, disliking emotional displays except in fiction. "Nonsense. You'd have found a way."

"I don't think so."

"Start teaching," she said. "Pass on what you've learned. Always pass it on."

She was an extraordinary teacher.

I believe that God put her in my life to assure me of my talent and help me refine it. Most of all, to encourage me.

I hope to be like her.[16]

I Am Encouraging and Supportive...

I take great joy in encouraging my students every day; and I am committed to always speak words that help, heal, cheer, and support. When I see my students growing and flourishing—not only academically, but personally—I will give the glory to God and be thankful for such an awesome opportunity. I am committed to supporting my students to pursue their dreams and reach for higher goals in the years to come.

A+

Incentive for Academic Achievement

Encourage your students to strive for higher academic marks by having small rewards available.

You might try filling six plastic eggs with small, inexpensive items like stickers, erasers, and small wrapped candy. In one of the eggs, include a free homework pass. Whenever students score 100 percent on a test, they have the opportunity to choose one egg. Whoever chooses the egg with the free homework pass is exempt from one assignment in the class in which he or she received the egg.

For example, if the student scores 100 percent in spelling, then the pass is good for one spelling assignment. The passes cannot be used for tests, quizzes, or review papers.

What student wouldn't want a homework pass! It may provide just the right incentive to motivate those students who have been lax in their work.[17]

More people fail for
lack of encouragement than
for any other reason.

ANONYMOUS

Who is not able to recall the impact
of some particular teacher—an enthusiast,
a devotee of a point of view,
a disciplinarian whose ardor came from love
of a subject, a playful but serious mind?
There are many images, and they are precious.

JEROME BRUNER
American Psychologist

Encourage one another and
build each other up,
just as in fact you are doing.

1 THESSALONIANS 5:11

Remember that happiness is a way of travel—not a destination.

ROY M. GOODMAN

New York Senator

Exceptional Teachers Are ...
Fun-loving and Joyful.

I really do believe I can accomplish
a great deal with a big grin.

BEVERLY SILLS

American Opera Singer

A Baby Shower for Miz Jones

I was barely twenty-two years old, straight out of college, and three months pregnant with my first child when I began my teaching career. With my army husband stationed elsewhere, the school system didn't ease my stress load when they assigned me to one of the roughest junior high schools in the city, where I taught Spanish and English. Vandalism was rampant, and there were often knife fights in the courtyard. Disruptive behavior in the classroom was the norm. Even so, I was excited about my first teaching assignment.

I was physically and mentally exhausted by the time I got home. At night I would do lesson plans, sew maternity clothes since I couldn't afford to buy them, and fall into bed. The next morning I would get up early, sit on the side of my bed for a nauseous moment, then run to the bathroom and throw up. My daily routine. Then I would face my students, trying desperately to reach them and meet their needs, managing to take a smile with me each day to class.

About six weeks into the school term, I could wait no longer to switch my wardrobe to maternity clothes. The girls noticed immediately. There were whispers and giggles then finally an outright question. "Miz Jones, are you gonna have a baby?"

I smiled and answered, "I certainly am."

What difference that made I don't know, but students began acting a little nicer. Even the boys were more polite, and the girls liked to hang around after class and ask questions. Now they knew why I sometimes went flying out of the classroom and ran down the hallway. They seemed genuinely concerned to find that I was throwing up in the bathroom due to the pregnancy.

Students took it upon themselves to chastise other students who caused me problems. No one was to bother Miz Jones because she was going to have a baby. Their tough hearts seemed to melt a little more each day.

When the semester ended, so did my teaching career for that year with only two months to go before the baby's due date. On my last day of school, the big, burly teacher from

across the hall detained me outside my classroom. This was unusual and I suddenly became suspicious. Had the kids done something awful? Why was he keeping me from entering my classroom?

Finally, I opened the door to a chorus of "Surprise!"

My students were ecstatic. They had a few wrapped presents on my desk and some treats approved by the principal when they told him they wanted to give me a surprise baby shower. The kids congregated around my desk to watch me open the small gifts of baby bibs, rubber pants, pacifiers, and such. There were cards with sweet sentiments, and no one wanted me to leave. "We'll never know if you had a girl or a boy," one student remarked. "We want to see the baby." I promised I would bring the baby to see them sometime the next semester.

True to my word, I took my baby boy to the school one spring afternoon and disrupted the class of students who had given me the baby shower. Everyone "oohed" and "aahed" over my precious bundle, and the students seemed genuinely touched that I had kept my promise.

My next teaching assignment took me to a high school on the other side of the city, so I never saw my junior high students again, though I thought of them often. No, I didn't wonder if they could speak Spanish fluently or get commas just right in English. I wondered if they remembered a very pregnant teacher who had loved them genuinely and hoped she had made a difference in their lives.

I also wondered if they had any idea what an impact they made on my own life. You see, after thirty-five years, I still have those "baby shower" cards scribbled with seventh-grade sentiments. And my baby boy? Well, he grew up and became a teacher![18]

What better place to express your zany side
than when you're in a classroom setting!
You're guaranteed to garner the attention of your
students—so don't hold back. Bring as much
joy and laughter into the classroom
as it can possibly contain.

🌴

A cheerful disposition is good for your health.

PROVERBS 17:22 MSG

Nutrition on the Go

Nourishing your body will provide much-needed energy to accomplish the many tasks you must perform each day. Try some of these ideas.

❀ *Prepare your meals the night before.*

Pack a lunch, even something quick and light such as a piece of fruit and some crackers. By doing this the night before, you will have one less thing to think about before hurrying out the door the next morning.

❀ *Keep a few packaged foods in your drawer.*

Fruits like oranges and apples can stay fresh in a drawer for several days. Granola bars offer a nutritious alternative to that candy from the vending machine and can give you a boost of energy. Even a package of instant oatmeal or soup in a coffee cup can be concealed while you rush off to your next engagement.

❀ *Keep extra change in your drawer for vending machines.*

You never know when you might be working late and will need an extra snack to tide you over. Choose the most nutritional item offered, and avoid sugary foods as much as possible.

❀ *If possible, have a small microwave and refrigerator in your room.*

These small appliances will come in very handy. Not only are they helpful for storing or heating up a lunch on the go, but they are also highly beneficial for class projects.[19]

Heavenly Father,

One of my greatest desires is to have fun with my students, to help them see that learning can be a joyful experience and not a drudgery. But sometimes my energy flags and my mind goes blank—and I feel like I'm completely out of creative ideas.

Help me, Father, to always exhibit Your joy, Your lightheartedness, Your complete delight in the tiniest details of everyday life. Just as I experience great joy as I learn from You, help me to bring that same spirit of fun and energy into my classroom each day. Your joy is our strength, Father. Help us to rejoice in You always!

Amen.

A+

Tulip the Clown

Our mission team had gone to a Publeto, in the high desert area of Mexico, to take spiritual and physical help, as well as hope to this very deprived group of people. Among the mission team members were doctors, dentists, an optical team, a pharmacist, and yes—a clown, named Tulip!

As people met with the medical staff, I began my role as Tulip—singing, making balloon animals, and telling Bible stories. Unfortunately, the only place available to me was a shaded area dividing lanes of traffic. The children sat in the shady area, and I stood in the street, moving for an occasional vehicle. We sang songs, I entertained, and at last I told a Bible story.

Noticing a large group of men gathering nearby, I began to feel a little apprehensive, but I stayed busy with the children, determined to keep a watchful eye. Then, as the growing group merged closer, I noticed that the men were attentively listening!

At the end of my story, the children lined up to receive their animal balloons and sweet treats. Meanwhile, one of the men who had been close by called out, "We want to know more about what the clown is saying."

That afternoon, several gave their hearts to God and received Spanish Bibles. One man, stating his eagerness for our return, offered his home for meetings. Two months later, we did return—to an established mission to hold weekly services!

What an honor it was to have had a part in the transformation of that small community. You see, as children of God, we are all teachers. And though it seems unlikely at times, someone is watching, listening, and hungering for a touch from God.[20]

Be on the lookout for someone who could use a joyful boost today. Smile; offer a word of affirmation or encouragement. You never know when the joy that radiates from you will offer a flicker of hope to a hungry heart searching for a touch from God.

I Am Fun-Loving and Joyful...

Because God has given me His joy, I can relax and have fun with my students. I am determined to make the classroom a place of adventure and wonder. And I am thankful that I serve a God who delights in the laughter of His children.

A+

THE FIRST DAY OF SCHOOL

The first day of school should be a time of fun and celebration! It will set the tone for the rest of the year.

🌲 *Recruit new-student escorts.*

New students usually struggle with the first few weeks of school. Having a returning student act as an ambassador to show the new students around the building, introduce them to people, and generally get them acquainted with the routine of the school can make adjustments less stressful.

🌲 *Write a letter to each student.*

Write a short but sincere letter of welcome to every student and place it on each desk along with a colorful pencil or eraser. Be sure to have extras on hand for those unexpected new students.

🌲 *State your expectations up front.*

Students work better when they know what is expected from them at the start. Go over the rules, systems, and your expectations for your class on the first day. Answering questions and sorting out any confusion will erase many unnecessary difficulties in the future. Consider asking the students what their expectations are of you. It can offer valuable insight that you might want to implement. This also helps the students feel that they are participating in the administration of their classroom.[21]

STRESS RELIEF

Try these strategies for a more peaceful life.

🌴 ***Get plenty of sleep.***

No one functions best when sleep deprived. Getting enough rest will not only help relieve stress, but it will also help you avoid that nasty cold that is going around.

🌴 ***Be on time.***

Consider setting your clock at home a couple of minutes ahead of the actual time to give yourself a psychological cushion.

🌴 ***Slow down.***

Purposely slow your breathing and take full breaths. Walk, talk, and drive at a slower pace. Life isn't a race.

🌴 ***Go in early to prepare for the day.***

Having to stop in the middle of class to find a book or make copies can be a hassle and breaks synergy with both the teacher and the students.

🌴 ***Kick off your shoes.***

Take a minute or two to kick off your shoes, lean your head back, and close your eyes. It will work miracles for you!

🌴 ***Invest in a comfortable chair.***

It's well worth the money to invest in a good, comfortable chair. Make sure to acquire one that will allow you to lean your head back for a moment of rest. It should also provide sufficient back support.[22]

That's what learning is. You suddenly understand something

you've understood all your life, but in a new way.

DORIS LESSING

British Writer

Exceptional Teachers Are ... Perceptive and Insightful.

🌴

Eyes that look are common,
eyes that see are rare.

Missionary Statesman and Bible Teacher
1902–1992

We shall not cease from exploration

And the end of all our exploring

Will be to arrive where we started

And know the place for the first time.

T. S. ELIOT

English Poet

1888–1965

You must look into people

as well as at them.

LORD CHESTERFIELD

English Writer and Statesman

1694–1773

Having insight into a student's life takes
supernatural help at times. Don't be afraid to ask God
for wisdom as you work to understand a student.
God knows the heart of your student better than
anyone else and desires to give you guidance.

🌳

The proverbs ... [are]
for attaining wisdom and discipline;
for understanding words of insight. ...
Let the wise listen and add to their learning,
and let the discerning get guidance.

PROVERBS 1:1–2, 5

Resolving Classroom Conflict

Unfortunately, conflicts are inevitable. By teaching your students to resolve their conflicts in a healthy manner, you are equipping them with a vital life skill that they can use for the rest of their lives.

✿ *Teach your students to resolve their conflicts.*

First, separate the offenders until they can cool off. Then have them write down five things they admire about the other person. They are to stay in class until they can read their lists sincerely and offer a handshake or hug. Of course, this works for older students, but the principle can even be applied to kindergartners.

✿ *Don't allow students to speak unkindly of other students or teachers.*

Invite violators to stand before the class and say five nice things about the person they have bad-mouthed.

✿ *Provide energy breaks.*

If a student is disruptive and having a hard time paying attention due to an overabundance of energy, have the student stand and, for a full minute, tell a joke, sing a song, or do a silly dance. When the minute is up, have the student return to his or her desk and give you and their studies their full attention for the rest of the period.[23]

Heavenly Father,

Some days, I feel inadequate to truly help my students. My knowledge of their lives is lacking—limited to what I see in the classroom each day.

I need Your insight, Father. You are well acquainted with the needs and desires of each student in my care. Thank You for the privilege of being in a position where I can have an impact on their lives. And thank You for Your quiet assurance that, as I turn to You for wisdom, You'll show me how I can best respond to each need.

Amen.

A+

Forgiven

I tried to read his expression as anger twisted my insides. He sat stone still, glaring at me.

"How could you have stolen the grade book?" I demanded.

No answer.

I wanted to impose a punishment that he wouldn't forget, but I sensed God wanted me to handle this a different way. I could see right through Jared's hollow defiance and was reminded of the many times I had failed. No matter how many times I had blown it, each time God had picked me up and forgiven me. I imagined myself sitting in Jared's chair, fearful of what punishment lay in store for my misdeeds.

I slowly sat down in front of him and said, "I forgive you."

"What?" came his surprised reply.

"I forgive you," I said again.

"What are you going to do to me?" he asked shakily.

"Absolutely nothing. You are free to go."

He looked at me, bewildered. "But I stole a grade book. Aren't you going to punish me?"

"Not this time. I am giving you an absolute pardon if you would like it."

He stared at me for a moment, then his eyes filled with tears. "Mrs. Pilgrim, I'm so sorry. I didn't want to steal the book, but the other boys were making fun of me."

"I understand peer pressure can be very difficult to handle," I said. "And I forgive you, but I ask that you never do anything like that again, okay?"

"I promise, Mrs. Pilgrim, never."

That day I learned an invaluable lesson—to look at my students the way God looks at us—individually. I learned not to react out of emotion, but to listen to God's Spirit within me, allowing Him to guide my actions. He knows the key to unlock every heart.[24]

Positive Strategies to Handle Difficult Students

Every teacher has war stories about problematic students. Develop strategies to turn difficult situations around.

❀ *Publicly verbalize the student's positive attributes.*

You may be the only person to offer encouraging words to him or her.

❀ *Assign "important" responsibilities.*

Giving the student an opportunity to excel in something and to receive positive feedback will help satisfy the need to act out for negative attention.

❀ *Document, document, document.*

Document everything, from what actions you take with the student to making copies of notes you send home to parents. You can never be too careful, and documentation could protect you from greater challenges down the road.

❀ *Establish a preassigned isolation area.*

Make this a place near you to which a disorderly student may be directed. This will help to minimize the problem without taking too much time away from instruction.

❀ *Get to the root of the problem.*

There is always a reason that a student acts out. Attempt to find the source of the problem as quickly as possible, and strive to eliminate or relieve it. The student's cry for negative attention could be a signal of a deeper issue. Keep an eye out for abuse or problems at home.[25]

DEVELOPING RAPPORT WITH YOUR STUDENTS AND THEIR PARENTS

The saying, "You catch more flies with honey than with vinegar," can be applied to the classroom. Try to achieve the best possible relationship with your students and their parents. Doing so will engender optimum cooperation.

* ***Write personal notes.***

    A simple note can brighten a child's day and form a bond between teacher and student. A note can also be sent home to parents, praising their child for a job well done.

* ***Return all calls promptly.***

    This will not only establish good rapport, it will be greatly appreciated.

* ***Keep in close contact with parents before a problem arises.***

    Parents like to hear that their child is doing well. Don't wait until there is a problem to contact them. Capture the opportunity to say, "Thank you," "Good job," "I noticed," "I understand," or "Good point." This will build a connection between you, the student, and the parents.

* ***Admit when you are wrong.***

    There is no better way to win the respect of your class than to openly and quickly admit when you are wrong.

🌸 ***Write positive notes on graded papers.***

Students value the notes that are written on their returned work. You never know; one of those papers could become a treasured possession.

🌸 ***Sit with students at lunch.***

Although it is nice to have some time away from your class, take the opportunity to sit with students at lunch once in a while. You will build trust and confidence with them if they feel you really care.

🌸 ***Attend your students' extracurricular activities.***

Children love to be supported in the activities in which they participate. Make a point to go to some of their after-school activities such as sporting events and music recitals.

🌸 ***Practice what you preach.***

Children want to feel that you are being fair. Make sure that you abide by the rules you enforce with your class.

🌸 ***Send notes that require a parent's signature.***

By having a specific place on assignments or notes where parents are to initial, you can quickly tell which parents have read the information and which ones might need a follow-up call.[26]

True patience is to suffer the wrongs done to us by others

in an unruffled spirit and without feeling resentment.

Patience bears with others because it loves them.

GREGORY THE GREAT

Catholic Pope

540–604

Exceptional Teachers Are ...
Persevering and Patient.

Patience and perseverance have a
magical effect before which difficulties
disappear and obstacles vanish.

JOHN QUINCY ADAMS
Sixth United States President
1767–1848

"Oh, for more patience!" may be the heart cry
of every teacher. When your own patience wanes,
turn to God; He'll give you the strength you need
to persevere and get the job done.

🌴

*[The LORD said:] "These things I plan won't happen
right away. Slowly, steadily, surely, the time approaches when
the vision will be fulfilled. If it seems slow, wait patiently,
for it will surely take place. It will not be delayed."*

HABAKKUK 2:3 NLT

Grading Made Easy

With enormous amounts of papers to grade, shortcuts and simple ideas to help with the grading process can keep things flowing smoothly.

🍀 **Institute and utilize answer columns.**

Having your students make answer columns on one side of their papers can make grading easier and faster for you. These columns are convenient for you to check—even multiple papers at a time—and if there is a question, you have the original problem right there to double-check.

🍀 **Assign student numbers.**

Giving students classroom numbers at the beginning of the year can make several processes flow easier. Have students put their number at the top of all their papers so you can quickly check and see if someone did not turn in work. The students can also walk in numerical order or reverse numerical order to recess and lunch. In addition, all textbooks can be marked with the student numbers, and you will know right away who is responsible for any books that might be missing during inventory.

🍀 **Combine assignments.**

To cut down on the number of pages to correct, try combining assignments. For example, spelling or vocabulary words can be used in a language-arts essay. If the spelling words are underlined, you can check them quickly and then read the essay. Then record both grades in the corresponding subjects.[27]

Heavenly Father,

Some days, I just want to scream! It seems the same old problems keep rearing their ugly heads—the same conflicts, the same name-calling. Am I really making progress with these kids? Am I affecting their lives for good? Some days, I just want to throw in the towel.

But I know, Father, that You never give up on me—even when I'm being cranky, selfish, and insensitive to others. Though You might be tempted to throw in the towel, You persevere. Your patience is limitless.

So please help me to be more like You, Father—more patient with these pupils. Give me the strength to persevere when I feel like I'm not seeing progress. And give me the patience to run the race with my students so that we might enjoy the rewards of a race well run together.
                                            Amen.

A+

Patience is the key to joy
companion of wisdom.

ST. AUGUSTINE
Philosopher and Bishop of Hippo
354–430

The fruit of the Spirit is ... patience.

GALATIANS 5:22

The two most powerful warriors
are patience and time.

LEO NIKOLAEVICH TOLSTOY
Russian Novelist and Philosopher
1828-1910

She Taught More than Music

My children's piano teacher never knew the impact she would make on my life. I remember the first time I spoke with her. She came highly recommended by a salesman at a local music store.

"If your children really want to learn, I will teach them," she said. "I am trying to slow down, but I cannot turn a pupil away if he is eager to learn. We will start next Monday."

All three children were excited. They thought Monday would never come. I bought the suggested music. After I picked them up from school, off we went for their very first lessons.

I was surprised when I saw the teacher. She was well into her senior years. Her fingers were bent with arthritis. She wore an exuberant smile and carried herself well. Her hair was pulled back into a tight bun. She had reserved three thirty-minute time slots for my children.

After I introduced my children, I left to do a little shopping. I returned to pick the kids up ahead of schedule. I wondered how she could continue to play the piano with the obvious pain in her arthritic hands. I didn't want to be late or to cause her to spend more time teaching than planned.

When I returned, she was in the process of teaching her second pupil. The first was doing his homework. The third was still patiently waiting. I sat down and glanced around her living room.

Everything was placed neatly on the waxed tables. Piano figurines sat on the end tables. A Bible was on her coffee table, along with several inspirational magazines. The ninety minutes turned out to be more like two and a half hours.

"You have three fine children," she announced. "I think that they will all do very well musically." I shook her hand and affirmed that we would return the next Monday. After the four of us got into the car, much chatter began. My children had fallen in love with the magic of music.

We went back for another afternoon filled with lessons the next Monday. Again, the hour and a half slipped into more than two hours. For weeks, the scenario was the same. I continued to return from my shopping trips early—just in case.

I found I was looking forward to the quiet times I spent in her living room. It gave me time to draw closer to God while I listened to my children play.

The lessons were reasonably priced in comparison to the other piano teachers' rates. I tried to pay her extra for each day's lessons.

"No, no," she explained. "I won't take a dime more than the agreed-upon fee."

"But you are spending a great deal of time with my children…"

Before I finished my sentence she chimed in, "Listen, honey. When I was a child, I took piano lessons. My teacher continuously cut my lessons short. I told the Lord that if He would allow me to learn to play the piano, I would give lessons as long as I possibly could. I promised God that I would give back to my students the extra time that my teacher took from me. That is the reason I continue to teach with these hands and the reason I teach longer than expected."

Many years have now passed. That sweet and remarkable piano teacher has since gone to be with the Lord. In measuring her time, this teacher never failed to show her true self. She gave more than she received while living here on earth. In the end, I am certain that this special teacher gained a much larger reward because of her generosity and sacrifice. She taught more than music.

Today, I believe that this special piano teacher is playing in heaven. Her hands are now healed, her smile is more joyful, and no doubt the angels are singing along.[28]

I Am Persevering and Patient...

Because of God's great patience with me, I can be patient with my students. I'm determined to breathe a little more slowly and release the difficult situations into God's able hands. I know that as I demonstrate patience with my students and persevere to reach a solution to challenges, they'll be inspired to do the same.

A+

EASING A DIFFICULT DAY

Inevitably you will be faced with a day that has been difficult and draining. Take a few moments to put aside the trials of the day and end it on a positive note.

🍀 *Keep an inspirational book in your drawer.*

Taking a few moments to read a passage in a book that inspires you can help to change the mood of the day.

🍀 *Listen to a book on tape.*

Use the commute home to listen to a tape or CD of that book you've been wanting to read.

🍀 *Call a friend who makes you laugh.*

Laughter is the best medicine to help you out of a slump. Find a way to make yourself laugh—it will lift your spirit and renew your strength.

🍀 *Take a bubble bath.*

Slip into a steaming bath with lots of bubbles and let your cares float away.

On a particularly challenging day, you may need to do all of these. Remember, tomorrow is a new day. You owe it to yourself and your students to begin it refreshed, replenished, and ready to go.

🌴 *Keep a folder with notes of appreciation.*

Keep a folder handy containing the notes of appreciation you receive from your students, their parents, and faculty members. It can bring a smile to your face and warmth to your heart.

🌴 *Take the scenic route home.*

It may take a little longer, but you will have the opportunity to appreciate the glory and beauty of God's creation.

🌴 *Treat yourself.*

Stop by the store and buy yourself a flower, a fun new soft drink, an aromatic candle, or that new outfit you've had your eye on. It's okay to reward yourself for a job well done.

🌴 *Get or even give a hug.*

Nothing feels better or is more comforting than the warmth of a hug from someone who cares. Even if you have to initiate it, hug someone. You're sure to get one in return.[29]

I am not a teacher but an awakener.

ROBERT FROST

Pulitzer Prize-Winning American Poet

1874–1963

Exceptional Teachers Are ... Inspiring and Influential.

A teacher affects eternity;
he can never tell
where his influence stops.

HENRY BROOKS ADAMS

American Writer

1838–1918

115

You have the ability to influence your students in ways no one else can. Every positive word you speak will be imprinted on their hearts forever. God gave you a special task when He called you to teach, knowing you would be a wonderful inspiration to your students. So be encouraged, knowing He has entrusted you with a very special responsibility.

🌴

Be an example to all ... in what you teach, in the way you live, in your love, your faith, and your purity.

1 TIMOTHY 4:12 NLT

The heart of a child is a scroll,
A page that is lovely and white;
And to it as fleeting years roll,
Come hands with a story to write.

Be ever so careful, O hand;
Write thou with a sanctified pen;
Thy story shall live in the land
For years in the doings of men.

It shall echo in circles of light,
Or lead to the death of a soul.
Give here but a message of right,
For the heart of a child is a scroll.

ANONYMOUS

WAYS TO RENEW THE CLASSROOM ENVIRONMENT

Just as the air in a room can become stale and heavy, the feel of the classroom can sometimes become stagnant. Breathe new life into your classroom with these simple yet effective ideas.

❧ *Decorate for the different seasons.*

Class project items make great decorations, eliminating the need for storage space for those masterpieces. Remember not to overdo it or spend too much of your valuable time on decorating. Students love to help, and it instills in them a sense of pride in their classroom.

❧ *Place plants in various spots around your classroom.*

Whether you bring them from home or grow some for a class project, plants add life, color, freshness, and much-needed oxygen to the atmosphere.

❧ *Make space for an aquarium.*

The gentle sounds of an aquarium can help calm disruptive students and add a sense of tranquility to your classroom. It doesn't have to be elaborate; a simple goldfish in a bowl will do. What more delightful way to observe and enjoy the beauty of God's aquatic creatures and at the same time brighten up that empty corner in your room.

✿ *Take your class for a walk around the building.*

What a surprising treat for your class! Take a few moments to take a short jaunt and enjoy the change of scenery. The fresh air and short break from studies will reenergize your students and help them to shake off any unproductive heaviness.

✿ *Teach a lesson outside.*

Have your class sit on the grass as you read them a story, or have an art lesson on sketching a tree. Whether you are teaching a lesson on nature or just needing a change of pace, both you and your students will feel revitalized and ready to tackle the next activity.

✿ *Play music.*

It is said that classical music stimulates brain function. Keep a CD player and an assortment of soothing music to play while your students do seatwork. Try upbeat music to energize the class for spring cleaning.

✿ *Don't get stuck in a rut.*

Don't limit yourself by becoming trapped in a daily routine. Spice up the day by changing things around, whether it's altering the usual order of events or simply modifying seating for an activity. Plan surprises for your students. If you are excited, they will be too.

✿ *Rearrange the furniture.*

Have students sit in groups or form a semicircle around the board. You can also create activity centers for various projects. Set aside a corner of the room to decorate with a couple of floor pillows or beanbag chairs to create an inviting reading area. Variety is the spice of life.[30]

Heavenly Father,

Oh, to be known as an inspirer! There can't be any greater calling than this: to influence my students in a positive, life-changing way. To help them see their potential and to inspire them to pursue their dreams.

Thank You, Father, for the privilege of teaching and touching these lives. You've entrusted me with their care; and it's truly an awesome responsibility. Thank You for molding me into the kind of person they can look up to and respect. Help me to inspire my students to reach for bigger and better things in their own lives and to never settle for anything less.

Amen.

A+

A Shining Example

She never won any awards, nor was she highly acclaimed in her field, but Coach Harrison was my hero. She was strong and supportive, and she believed in me.

I began playing basketball in the seventh grade. I was awkward and had no idea what to do on the court, but Coach Harrison was there. She taught me the rules and the basics and instilled in me the love for athletics. She was there urging me on when I wanted to throw in the towel. She was there to support me when I was angry and hurt. She was there to push me to the next level when I refused to push myself.

Coach Harrison was more than just a coach; she was an example of what a teacher is supposed to be—someone to help you when you fall down, someone to challenge you to make it to the finish line, someone you can look up to and respect.

Insisting on excellence, she never allowed us to play dirty, to take cheap shots, or to bad-mouth the other team. To her, it really was about how you played the game. Coach Harrison taught me many things over the years, but the most important ones were how to be a respectable person, to play fair, to play hard, and to always give 110 percent. She instilled these values in us not just to be used in the game of basketball, but also to apply in life.

Today I coach basketball teams myself and often reflect on my time with Coach Harrison. I try to inspire my players just as she inspired me, to challenge them to push themselves to become better athletes, stronger individuals. I thank God for bringing Coach Harrison into my life. Because of her inspiration and influence, I am a better person today.[31]

I Am Inspiring and Influential...

Because I realize that God has given me the opportunity to inspire my students, I am committed to speak good and positive things into their lives. I'm mindful that my influence may be long lasting, and I will take my role seriously. I will take full advantage of this God-given opportunity to have an impact on the lives of my students in powerful, meaningful ways.

A+

The mediocre teacher tells.

The good teacher explains.

The superior teacher demonstrates.

The great teacher inspires.

WILLIAM A. WARD

American Teacher, Pastor, Author, and Editor

1921–1994

The fundamental qualification
for teaching is learning.

ANDREW MCNAB

No teacher should strive to make men think as he thinks,
but to lead them to the living Truth, to the Master himself,
of whom alone they can learn anything.

GEORGE MACDONALD
Scottish Minister and Writer
1824–1905

ENDNOTES

1. Amanda Pilgrim, "Effective Bulletin Boards." Used by permission of the author.
2. Darla Satterfield Davis, "Hidden Talents." Used by permission of the author.
3. Darla Davis, "Ways to Renew Your Spirit." Used by permission of the author.
4. Amanda Pilgrim, "Engaging Students in Classroom Participation." Used by permission of the author.
5. Darla Davis, "A Tough Little Philly in Texas." Used by permission of the author.
6. Debbie C. Justus, "Tips for Successful Parent/Teacher Conferences." Used by permission of the author.
7. Amanda Pilgrim, "Wise Ways to Simplify Your Life." Used by permission of the author.
8. Amanda Pilgrim, "Classroom Management." Used by permission of the author.
9. Amanda Pilgrim, "Learning to Trust Again." Used by permission of the author.
10. Debbie C. Justus, "Setting the Standard." Used by permission of the author.
11. Debbie C. Justus, "Recharging Your Batteries." Used by permission of the author.
12. Noelle Roso, "A Day to Treasure." Used by permission of the author.
13. Darla Davis, "Organizational Aids." Used by permission of the author.
14. Debbie C. Justus, "Bringing the Classroom to Life." Used by permission of the author.
15. Amanda Pilgrim, "Celebrating the Gifts and Strengths of Your Students." Used by permission of the author.
16. Elaine L. Schulte, "Zola Helen Ross: An Expert and an Encourager." Used by permission of the author.
17. Amanda Pilgrim, "Incentive for Academic Achievement." Used by permission of the author.
18. Louise Tucker Jones, "A Baby Shower for Miz Jones." Used by permission of the author.
19. Debbie C. Justus, "Nutrition on the Go." Used by permission of the author.
20. Cleo Justus, "Tulip the Clown." Used by permission of the author.
21. Amanda Pilgrim, "The First Day of School." Used by permission of the author.
22. Amanda Pilgrim, "Stress Relief." Used by permission of the author.
23. Debbie C. Justus, "Resolving Classroom Conflict." Used by permission of the author.
24. Amanda Pilgrim, "Forgiven." Used by permission of the author.
25. Debbie C. Justus, "Positive Strategies to Handle Difficult Students." Used by permission of the author.
26. Amanda Pilgrim, "Developing Rapport with Your Students and Their Parents." Used by permission of the author.
27. Amanda Pilgrim, "Grading Made Easy." Used by permission of the author.
28. Nancy B. Gibbs, "She Taught More Than Music." Used by permission of the author.
29. Debbie C. Justus, "Easing a Difficult Day." Used by permission of the author.
30. Debbie C. Justus, "Ways to Renew the Classroom Environment." Used by permission of the author.
31. Amanda Pilgrim, "A Shining Example." Used by permission of the author.

This and other titles in the Celebration Series
are available from your local bookstore.

Celebrate Dads
Celebrate the Graduate
Celebrate Love
Celebrate Moms

If this book has touched your life,
we would love to hear from you.
Please send your comments to:
editorialdept@whitestonebooks.com

Visit our Web site at:
www.whitestonebooks.com

*"... To him who overcomes I will give some of the hidden manna to
eat. And I will give him a white stone, and on the stone a new name
written which no one knows except him who receives it."*

REVELATION 2:17 NKJV

WHITE STONE BOOKS
LAKELAND, FLORIDA